Furth

Earthling

"More than any poet of his generation, Longenbach adventures a cleanly and generous ambition for the art, constantly mindful of his subject as Matter beyond occasion—Matter to be reverenced and thereby understood. In *Earthling*, he touches upon glory. His 'Allegory' is the finest instance of transcendence in American writing since Ammons's 'Easter Morning.' Every page of this collection merits permanence, a pleasure truly modern now."　　　　　　　　　—Donald Revell

"*Earthling* stuns me with its clarities, it fascinates me to no end. Is it Longenbach's passionate precision? Is it his absolute unmixed attentiveness that's akin to prayer? To my mind, *Earthling* is far more than just another brilliant, elegant book of verse: this is elegance at the edge of the abyss. This is a human voice that has come to the middle of life's desert to find that 'In the middle of the desert / you might be anyone.' Longenbach finds here the crystalline, transformative, pure pitch of a lyric poet: his voice in this book becomes any earthling's voice. How does he do it? How does he give clarity to the human in us? In another century people used to call this effect *visionary* work: the poetry of a true mystic."　　　　　　—Ilya Kaminsky

"James Longenbach knows as much about how poems work as anyone in the world, but he hides this knowledge behind poems that feel so real and artless they hardly seem composed at all. The poems in *Earthling* are mythological in their simplicity, and their myth is the inevitable one of an isolated consciousness inhabiting places that might or might not be actual, 'Moments when the artist in each of use created / The material world by finding the unfamiliar in the familiar.'"   —John Koethe

Earthling

Earthling

poems

JAMES LONGENBACH

W. W. NORTON & COMPANY

Independent Publishers Since 1923

New York | London

For information about permission to reproduce selections from this book,
write to Permissions, W. W. Norton & Company, Inc.,
500 Fifth Avenue, New York, NY 10110

For information about special discounts for bulk purchases, please contact
W. W. Norton Special Sales at specialsales@wwnorton.com or 800-233-4830

Manufacturing by Berryville Graphics
Book design by Chris Welch
Production manager: Lauren Abbate

Library of Congress Cataloging-in-Publication Data

Names: Longenbach, James, author.
Title: Earthling : poems / James Longenbach.
Description: First edition. | New York : W. W. Norton & Company, [2018]
Identifiers: LCCN 2017015728 | ISBN 9780393353433 (pbk.)
Classification: LCC PS3562.O4967 A6 2018 | DDC 811/.54—dc23
LC record available at https://lccn.loc.gov/2017015728

W. W. Norton & Company, Inc.
500 Fifth Avenue, New York, N.Y. 10110
www.wwnorton.com

W. W. Norton & Company Ltd.
15 Carlisle Street, London W1D 3BS

1 2 3 4 5 6 7 8 9 0

for Joanna, Kathryn, and Alice

Contents

I

II

III

IV

Earthling

Earthling, *noun.*

Forms: *irþling, yrþling, ærðling, eorðling.*

1. A ploughman, a cultivator of the soil.

2. A kind of bird (not identified).

I

SUITCASE

No one can predict the size, the shape, or even the location
Of the room where you will live a long time,
But every time you pack
You're thinking about that room.

You're imagining the color of the draperies,
You're deciding the desk should face the window in summer,
When the sun is overhead,
But face the wall in winter,
When the light's so low it hits you in the eyes.

In winter there are no distractions, you study the wall.
But in summer the trolley stops in front of the Ministry of
Public Instruction.

Usually it sits there, nobody moves, but sometimes
It's crossing the river.
Little houses, new apartments,
Bodies smelling fresh in the morning, rank at night—

When I pack, I lay out every sock, each pair
Of shorts without a fold.
If my shirts are too large to lie down flat,
I tuck their arms beneath their sides to fill the suitcase perfectly.
A window, the desk, a lamp and a chair.

One of life's greatest pleasures,
If I'm allowed the phrase,
Is packing a suitcase.

It's not like building a fire,
When you want to leave space for air.

COMPLAINT

Walk out the front door, the dog tugs
Boyishly at the leash.
I sit at my desk. A breeze
Floats up from Oakdale on the hottest day of the year.
This is the climate of reason.

But in the climate of no reason
I look out the window at midnight.
My mother appears in a red coat, raking the leaves.

Always she wore that coat in autumn,
The tattered wool, the large
Black buttons, but only to rake leaves.

Walk out the front door, somebody dies.
Walk out the back,
The rabbit jumps out of its hole.
Kitchen in one world, bedroom in another—

You could say it's always
September here,
Too warm, then cold,
Every day the first day of school.

The bus is waiting.
I've got books, my lunch,
My gym clothes in a plastic bag.

THE CROCODILE

1.

What I wanted was to lift my body in unnatural postures
High above the earth, to dance,
To live beyond ideas.
Imagine feeling assured you were beautiful.
Girls wanted to run their fingers on my skin, also guys; I bit off
   their hands.

If called to, I could wait beneath the water a long time.
I could let a bird pick leeches from my tongue.

So in the moment of youth when other people embrace passion
I fell back on discipline. My throat
Was capable of many different sounds but the pleasure
Was in keeping silent, letting parts of me be seen.
Sometimes a plover mistook me for a log
But that's not deception; I really look like a log.

I survived the great extinctions,
I pretended to be myself.
To let you know me, I need only move my eyes.

2.

Like me, you had a father and a mother,
You grew up in a particular place, a particular time.
Your skin displays the scars of that place.

You've decapitated chickens, eviscerated live fish.
You carry yourself with what, to other people, seems aplomb,
But the impulse driving such behaviors,
Necessary in themselves, has infiltrated daily life. In arguments
You'll drag another person underwater till he drowns.

Though I grew very large, though I developed great capacity of mind,
I was afraid of my mother. Afraid not just of scrutiny
But of being the object of someone's pride.
What was I protecting?
She was willful, yes,
But tiny, generous to a fault.

In Egypt, the family crocodiles were adorned
With bracelets, earrings of molten gold.
Then mummified, laid out in the tombs.
The word itself is from the Greek:
Krokodeilus, pebble worm.

3.

What manner of thing is your crocodile?

•

It is shaped, sir, like itself, and it is as broad as it has breadth;
it is just so high as it is, and moves with its own organs. It lives
by that which nourishes it, and the elements once out of it, it
transmigrates.

•

What color is it of?

•

Of its own color, too.

•

'Tis a strange serpent.

•

'Tis so, and the tears of it are wet.

—*Antony and Cleopatra*, II.7

23

4.

As a child, I was given a stuffed crocodile.
Don't think this strange; most humans have dolls resembling
    themselves.
My sister had one, too.

Tiny marbles filled the sockets of its eyes.
The skin was stitched together up the belly, where it's soft,
And though it was only a foot, perhaps ten inches long,
The jaws were clamped together with a tack.

Presumably this kept the little row of teeth from hurting you,
But the tack protruded from the bottom of its chin,
Sharper than any tooth.
I remember rubbing over it, back and forth.

When my mother died,
I was right beside her.
She'd been unconscious for a day.
My sister and my father were there, too.

I leaned down close to her left ear, I whispered,
Thank you for everything you did for me,
Thank you especially for what you did for our girls.

Then, immediately, the color left her face,
She was no longer in her body,
And she sank beneath the lagoon.

5.

Picture, by way of analogy, a mountain range.
Some interruption of traffic, perhaps a flood, has blocked the roads,
But communication between the villages is maintained over steep
   footpaths,
The kind used ordinarily by hunters, originally by their prey.

Some people speak more openly by inefficient means.
And the steeper the path, the more
Arduous the climb,
The more likely we are to believe.

Someday I won't be hungry.
I'll watch an egret stepping through the reeds.

The miser imagines there's a certain sum to fill his heart
But for sorrow there's no remedy.
It requires what it cannot hope.
We've known each other, earth, a long time.

When the light rests low on the Nile, the Ganges, the Everglades—
I could be anywhere—
Day is discontinued, motionless.
A voice is what you have.

THE DISHWASHER

For many years I saved my money, bought a car, a used Chevette.
Lean on me, said the radio, *when you're not strong.*

I'd known that song since I was young but every time I heard it
I wanted to hear it again.
I drove to the supermarket, then drove home.
I looked in the refrigerator, under the bed.

As if I were standing in the kitchen, unloading the dishwasher,
  holding the phone,
I heard my mother's voice.
I heard it plainly, as if she were standing in the room.

I know it's early, she said,
But I'm planning ahead for Christmas.

So I'd like to remember: What kind of coffee do you like?
Regular, or decaf, or both at certain times?
I want to be prepared, in case you'd like a cup when you're here.

BOOK THREE

Long ago, before you were born,
I lived in a house at the edge of a forest.
It was a yellow house; you've heard me speak of it before.
Much of what happened in the house was interesting, even
   amusing,
But at times I felt weighed down by a sadness

•

Impossible to overcome,
As if I lived at the bottom of a dark pit,
No prospect but a slender aspen tree against the sky.
Languidly, but not idly, one morning I began to draw the tree.
Its lines insisted upon being followed,

•

And as one branch rose from another, finding its place
In the air, the tree became more beautiful.
By laws finer than any known to me
The tree composed itself,
And when at last it was there in front of me, looking back,

•

Everything I'd ever thought about trees had disappeared.
As for the pit, the furies, the snakes,
The gloomy caverns and the burning lakes,
And last, and most, if these were cast behind,
The avenging horror of a conscious mind—

.

They neither are, nor were, nor ever can be
(Lucretius, *On the Nature of Things*, Book III).
All my life I prayed I'd die quickly.
But if death were but the absence of consciousness,
Like a long sleep unbroken by dreams,

.

I wouldn't be able to see you; neither
Could you hear me speak.
You're looking out the window, your feet on a chair.
Anyone who didn't know you would presume
You're waiting for something to happen

.

But in fact it's happening now.

II

BY THE SAME AUTHOR

Today, no matter if it rains,
It's time to follow the path into the forest.

The same people will be walking the same dogs,
Or if not the same dogs, dogs that behave in similar fashions,
Some barking, some standing aloof.
The owners carry plastic bags.

But this is the forest, they complain, we must do as we like.
We must let the dogs run free,
We must follow their example,
The way we did when we were young.

Back then we slept, watched TV—
We were the dogs.
By the time the screen door slammed, we were gone.

Nobody really talks like that in the forest.
They're proud of their dogs,
Proud especially of the ones who never bark.
They're upset about the Norway maple, it's everywhere,
Crowding out the hickories and oaks.

Did you know it takes a million seeds to make one tree?
Your chances of surviving in the forest,
Of replicating yourself, are slim.

Today, the smaller dogs are wearing raincoats,
The bigger ones are stiffing it out.
They're tense, preoccupied,
Running in circles,
Getting tangled in the leash.

It's hard remaining human in the forest.
To move the limbs of the body,
To speak intelligible words,
These things promise change.

SILVER SWAN

The streets were old, but all the people were young,
Striding forward with great purpose,
Girls smiling openly in the faces of boys.

Not every boy noticed, but we all kept walking forward,
Over the bridges, under the trees,
Streets not growing wider
But the buildings growing taller, taller than the trees,
And not just taller but more mannered, ornamental, asking
    also to be seen.

How did this happen? Where were our parents, our teachers,
People who long before us had worn
Footpaths into roads, roads into thoroughfares?

We walked to the park, to the station,
Skin beneath our sideburns soft as a girl's.
We watched the swan's nest growing larger
Though we never saw the swan build anything.

It sat along the riverbank or floated placidly across the water
Like a Schubert song, the tenor unaware
Of the piano beneath, the left hand
Indistinguishable from the right—

In time, we observed in one another a sadness,
Not bitter, a resignation
That made our actions, no matter
How many times we repeated them, feel complete.

ARCADIA

1.

Just as there were reeds along the riverbank,
Just as there were clouds
Above my head, my lute was lying beside me on the grass.

I placed the little finger of my right hand on the soundboard,
Just below the strings.
Not the tip of the finger, the side.

I curled the palm of my right hand toward me,
Covering the strings, so that I played
The bass note with the thumb,
The next with the index,
And the top note with the third.

The sun retreated, the night turned cold.
Rain began to fall, softly at first,
Though surely rain had fallen here before, as rain falls
    everywhere.

With my left hand, I positioned my thumb and index finger
Opposite each other, bearing no weight,
As if the neck of the lute were not there.

2.

At this they all laughed.

Then the Count began afresh: My lords, he said, I am not pleased if the young man is not also a musician, and if, besides his cunning upon the book, he have not skill in like manner on sundry instruments. There is no ease of labor more honest and more praise-worthy, especially at court, where many things are taken in hand to please women, whose tender breasts are soon pierced with melody.

Then the Lord Gasper: I believe music, he said, together with other vanities, is mete for women, also for them that have the likeness of men, but not for them that be men indeed, who ought not with such delicacies womanize their minds and so bring themselves to dread death.

—The First Booke of the Courtyer of
Count Baldessar Castilio

3.

For many years I lived apart, in happy oblivion.
In retrospect, I understand I'd been a child,
Though lacking comparisons I couldn't have said so.

I learned things, things no child, left to himself, could possibly know.
My head, which had been empty, now was full.

My head would grow larger.
How could it not?

At night, standing in the shower, I closed my eyes.
The water trickled down my forehead
To my nose, from my nose to my lips, my chin, then disappeared.

But some of what stayed in my head
Should not have been there.

4.

Listen, said the reeds along the riverbank: the nymphs
Are weeping for Daphnis.
His mother embraces his body, railing against the stars.

Nobody drives his cattle to the cool stream, no one could drink;
The mountains echo with the beasts of the desert.

Daphnis, it was you who yoked them to the chariot,
Who led us in the dance, weaving
Together vine leaves with reeds.

The vine exceeds the tree on which it climbs.
The grape exceeds the vine,
The calf the herd, the corn the field.

Now, where we planted barley, thistles grow.
Where once were violets, hyacinths—nothing but weeds.

Scatter the ground with flowers, shepherds,
Set out two bowls,
One of milk and one of oil.
Then carve these verses on his tomb.

5.

When I painted, everybody saw.
When I played, everybody heard.

I ate your raspberries.
The sign *No Trespassing* applied to me.

Now, the hemlocks have grown higher than the house.
There's moss on my stoop, a little mildew
In the shower but you've never seen my shower.

I can undress by the window,
I can sleep in the barn.

The sky, which is cloudy,
Suits the earth to which it belongs.

EARTHLING

Above our heads they're making pies.
They're cutting butter
Into tiny pieces, they're discussing its advantages over lard.

Together we will sit around the table
And the servings will be generous, first the apple, then the
   pumpkin—

Do we have to eat now?

I can smell the nutmeg.
I can hear the flour sifting to the bowl.

PETITE MAISON

In the village was a bar, a bistro, you might say,
Though really it was someone's home.
In the kitchen I could see a stove
No larger than our own,
And by the time we ordered

.

There was no more chicken, only lamb;
The locals ate there every night.
The next morning we walked to the market.
We filled our satchels not only
With fruits and vegetables

.

But with oils, spices, a set of wooden spoons.
We scrubbed our refrigerator,
We bought more food than it could hold.
But at the end of the day it was not fatigue
That returned us to the bar,

.

It was habit, as if we'd lived in the village all our lives.
Probably we lingered over the wine,
Surely we walked home,
The leaves would have been turning, it was September,
The moon a little dollop of red fire—

                    •

I realize that all my life I rarely
Spoke this way; nihilism
Was my defense against the glamour of fortitude.
But in the paths of creation, in the darkness and the light,
Things seem bad when really

                    •

They're at variance with other things.
With things we may not see
They're in accord.
Then they are good; in themselves, too, they are good.
The next morning, when we awoke

                    •

To find the bar was gone, the shutters closed,
The few chairs scattered at the curb,
I asked the earth if we should stay here, make this our home.
Earth said you must never leave,
You must stay here forever.

ALLEGORY

1.

In the Forest of Wearisome Sadness,
Where often I've found myself wandering alone,
I met my heart, who called to me, asking me where I was going.

The path was long and straight, row after row of conifers
    receding
To a horizon that because of the geometry
Seemed farther than it really was,
Like the door at the top of a staircase in Versailles.

But as if the forest's maker had been offended by elegance,
A pile of rocks disrupted the rows: the forest once
Had been a field. I remember that field.

I was carried there by my father, beside him
My grandfather, who planted the trees.
Until they were tall enough to survive,
He mowed the field, piling up rocks, taking down brush with a
    scythe.

How, since I've known the forest almost since birth, could I
    have been lost?
Why, since the forest is beautiful, is it not a place of delight?

Repeatedly I asked these questions of my heart,
But like a good physician, he elected
To keep silent, leaving me to answer for myself.

2.

Late at night, when I'm lying in bed and cannot sleep,
My heart reads to me from the Romance of Pleasant Thought.
Always I've heard the story before, and typically,
Since the stories are true, I am their hero.

I'm riding my tricycle on the sidewalk near the house where I was
  born.
Because I am unsupervised, I indulge in what seems at the
  moment
A daring wish: I ride the tricycle beneath a sprinkler.

Immediately I am overcome with remorse.
Evidence of my trespass is everywhere to be seen,
And for the first time in my life I contemplate a lie.

Would my shirt dry faster if I stood in the sun, where it's hot,
Or in the shade, where cool breezes rustle the leaves?

In the version of this story that appears now
In the Romance of Pleasant Thought,
I admire not so much my ingenuity
As the evidence of my early devotion to empiricism,
The way I manage terror by examining how things work.

3.

It's done, there's nothing more to say.
My heart is gone from me.
Because he has fallen in love
He has abandoned me.

It's pointless making myself uncomfortable over this
By being mournful or sad.
It's done, there's nothing more to say.
My heart is gone from me.

He does nothing but mock me.
When I tell him pitifully
That I cannot live on my own,
He does not listen.
It's done, there's nothing more to say.

—after Charles d'Orléans

4.

Imagine you've been in love forever, since before you were born.
You walk the field. At every third step
You scoop out a handful of wheat
From the seed bag, scattering it broadcast.
As the sun comes up you're walking in a golden cloud.

Inside the cloud, time no longer exists.
Your back's not bent, your body is a boy's.

Outside, since it's time for wheat,
The summer rains are finished.
Otherwise it's oats. Every third year it's clover.

The advantage to people like you,
Though there are many disadvantages, is this:
When the earth no longer needs what you can grow,
You plant hundreds, then thousands
Of seedlings, conifers, trees that bear no edible fruit.

Do not imagine yourself sad; you are a servant,
Guided by a fate much more substantial than your own.

You arrange the trees in rows, you tend them,
You're proud of them.
You watch the forest reappear.

LYRIC KNOWLEDGE

Finally having cleaned out the closet, I awoke
To find it filled with things.
Somebody else might need those things,
So I put them in a box, I put the box at the curb.

The following morning, after breakfast, the closet once again
    was full.
Once again I cleaned it, this time retaining things
Unfamiliar to me, discarding the rest.

In my mind, these acts of accumulation transpired
As quickly as the acts of dispersal,
A single night, a single day.
In fact they took many years.

In one of those years I wrote a book.
Rather than discarding things
Outright, I redeployed them, altering their function.

But at the end of the year I nonetheless found myself at the curb.
I greeted my neighbors, I was greeted in turn.

Together we watched the cars go by.
The cars followed the road. Above our heads
The leaves turned silver in the breeze.

PREFACE TO AN UNWRITTEN BOOK

Probably you never noticed the portrait
Hanging beside the stairs:
A young woman, though now she'd be about my age.
I had it painted when she died.
Somehow in the fifty years since then

.

This house has grown up around her,
The few books written,
The many I've read.
But in summer, in early evening,
There's really nothing I'd rather do

.

Than sit here on the stairs.
We work in the dark,
As Henry James once said,
We do what we can, we give what we have.
As for the book I'm supposed to be writing now—

.

If you think I should do it, Jim, I will.

But you should realize I'd much rather spend my time

Reading or, since it's the end

Of summer, sitting.

Our truest impulses are so immature

.

That most of us can't recognize them,

Much less have the fortitude

To carry them out.

I've needed to remain

Mysterious, even to me.

CLIMATE OF REASON

1.

Whenever I find myself growing grim about the mouth,
Whenever it is a drizzly November in my soul,
I get myself to the desert,
Where there is only rock and sand.

Just thinking about it, making sentences
About it, some of the words
Borrowed, some of them my own, is almost enough.
I bring a water bottle and a book.

At this point, the same thing always happens: I pour the
    water on the ground.
As quickly as it leaves the bottle,
Glistening for a moment in sunlight, the water evaporates.

Sometimes I spend the night there, curled up on the sand.
I imagine the beasts of the desert
Circling me, lions and wolves protecting me.

But most nights I return to the house from which I came.
I sleep in a bed where recently another man died.
A headboard, two pillows, a quilt
That someone long ago stitched by hand.
My mother stitched quilts by hand.

When I return to the desert the next morning,
A tree has grown up where I poured the water.
All day I sit beneath the branches.

2.

Enfeebled by prolonged fasting,
The hermit is unable to concentrate on holy things.

His thoughts wander. Memories of his past
Evoke regrets he can no longer suppress,
And as memory begets memory,
He turns ever more deeply into himself.

He rehearses his flight from home, his mother, her perfume.
He remembers his visit to Alexandria,
The slender bodies of both girls and boys.

Involuntarily he yields to the dissatisfaction growing inside him.
Grace departs from him; hope burns low in his heart.

He dreams of the Maccabees slaughtering their enemies
And desires that he might do likewise
With the Alexandrians.
He indulges in reveries concerning the riches of biblical kings.

The Sphinx, the Chimera, all the abnormalities
Described by Herodotus he beholds.
Grotesqueries made animate,
A Sabbath of abominations—

As if everything inside him had spoiled.

Sand-drifts follow the course of the winds,
Rising and falling like great shrouds.

3.

I could go on like this; there's nothing in the desert but time.
Time to read, to think, but mostly
Time to read nothing, to think about nothing.

You go there encumbered, needing to be alone,
And in almost no time you're lonely, which is what you want,
But also what you dread, the landscape stretching far as you can see.

Nothing but rubble. Mountains
In the distance red against a cobalt sky.

One minute you're sharing a good bottle of wine,
You're eating tortelloni stuffed with ricotta and pear,
A little sautéed kale on the side.

Then you're in the desert,
There's work to do.

The desert says
Study that tree,
What is it like?

A silly old man.

4.

A certain man, revered by the Fathers,
Was living in the desert of Porphyrio.
For sustenance he had a date palm over his head, a small garden
   at his feet.
When the date palm sprouted new branches,
He collected the dead ones, thinking they might someday be of use.

Have you ever lived alone a long time?
Then you know that for the hours when the sun appears
Unmoving, directly overhead,
This man was beset with fatigue, as if recovering from a long
   journey.

He turned his head anxiously, first to the left, then to the right,
To see if anyone approached.
He called to the beasts
Of the desert, that they might return.

No one to talk to. Nothing to see.
So while it was a journey of seven days to the nearest city,
Making the conveyance of his handiwork more costly
Than the sum such handiwork might fetch,
He began to weave baskets,
Slowly at first, then with great dexterity.

The brighter the sunlight,
The more intricate his designs.

The date palm dropped more branches,
The days passed quickly as the nights.
And at the end of the year, when his hut was filled to capacity,
He burned the baskets,
Mixing the ashes into the soil.

5.

Song of the Desert

Once I was a girl, I fell in love. Against my better judgment
I allowed myself to fall in love.

Then I was not

A girl, I was the earth.
Pour me a glass of water, once I was the sea.

6.

Song of the Basket

Had you permitted it, earth,
I would have loved
You like a little bird
That picks up crumbs.

7.

Essentially, an artist's work consists of giving life
To the dead matter of the material world.
That matter is the artist's medium.

The artist is in love with it.
He may, as lovers do,
Selfishly expect that what he loves loves him.

But if the artist loves the medium enough to submit to its
    real qualities,
Refusing to exaggerate how they might please him,
The result may justify his idealization.

Such artists fear not so much boredom
As work without pleasure.
In fact, if their work is to succeed,
They require boredom.
They must wait for its effect.

Moments when the artist in each of us created
The material world by finding the unfamiliar in the familiar,
By finding what we'd never known to be ourselves
In what seemed dead—
Such moments are forgotten by most people.

Or else they're guarded in a secret place of memory,
Too much like visitations of the gods
To be mixed with everyday thinking.

8.

Before there was the tree, there was the house.
Before the house, the bed,
Before the bed, the quilt.

I could have stayed in the desert forever,
Except I was hungry, I had to eat.

So I returned to the house, I made a sandwich.
Don was in the kitchen; Claudia was reading on the deck.
A rabbit skittered once, then twice, then laid its ears against
    its head.

In the middle of the desert
You might be anyone,
Except you're never in the middle,
You're at the edge.

Then you're yourself again.
You look in the mirror,
It's like magic. There you are.

IV

HUNTINGTON MEADOW

Though I come from a long line of people intimate
With the bodies of horses,
Today, for the first time, I touched a horse.
I placed my hand on its left flank, just behind the shoulder.
The horse was standing beside me, eating grass.

I'm speaking here of things that come to feel essential
Though they happen at one moment in time.
You've never done it, then you've done it before, you're good at it.
You can't imagine your body without it.

Tanqueray up with an olive,
Nobody home, the brine
Still unexpected at the bottom of the glass.

When I touched the horse, I didn't move my hand.
The hide more skin than hair,
The muscle beneath it visceral, relaxed,
More like a lover's than a dog's.

Then, after I took my hand away, I immediately put it back.
The horse seemed all the while
Perfectly happy, ripping up grass at the roots.

That was the only sound, the sound
You hear when you're gardening, weeding the lawn,
Somebody right there beside you, also weeding,
Though because you lack nothing
You're also completely alone.

THE HUMMINGBIRD

Sunlight, food, and daily exercise produced
In me the body of an adult.
The attributes that made other adults attractive,
Though I was slow to acknowledge them, I recognized in myself.

I positioned myself in the morning light, just so.
I cruised the bottlebrush, birds-of-paradise,
And though I was still hungry
I came as close to the glass without touching as custom allows.

When you're ruled by your body, condemned
Each day to fill it so that tomorrow
You might fill it again,
Nothing is more erotic
Than a room without flowers.

In the *Phaedo*, after Socrates drinks the poison,
He walks around the house until his legs become heavy.
Then he lies down on his back.
He touches his feet,
Then touches his ankles, his shins.

When the cold has risen as far as his abdomen
He throws the sheet from his face.
Criton, he says, we owe a cock to Asclepios,
God of healing. Pay it without fail.

THE ACADEMY

Reluctantly, having returned to the very neighborhood
I'd once called home, I was staying at a small hotel.
I tied my tie, untied it, then tied it again.
I took the elevator to the lobby, exited
The revolving door, but the longer I walked

.

The less attention I paid to detail.
The city's accretions, the shops, the people who frequented them,
No longer distracted me from the underlying contour of earth,
Which rose precipitously, then fell away,
So that just by walking forward, walking straight,

.

Suddenly I saw for miles, and then,
Without adjusting my goal, saw only my feet.
One minute I stood at the edge of a great escarpment,
    overlooking the sea.
Then rocks I'd climbed gave way to a level plain,
There were fields of lavender, and in the distance

.

What appeared to be a monastery perched at the top of a hill.
I took off my jacket, I loosened my tie;
I was anxious about getting lost.
But time had taught me only too well
The impossibility of attaining in the world

•

The world I'd known, as Proust says in *The Past Recaptured*.
He's at the party at the house of the princess, it's been a long
    journey,
And he speaks of himself, unthinkingly,
As a young man, which makes everybody laugh.
When I arrived at the Academy at the top of the hill

•

I found my place card, took my seat.
I ate the appetizer, then the main course, and like everyone
I endured the ceremony at which many names
Were called, including finally my own.
The phrase *a young man* is one my mother might have used,

•

My mother for whom I was still always a child.
And if, as I heard my name, I registered certain changes
Which had taken place since childhood,
I judged them from the perspective she did,
One thing having followed another

.

Unpredictably, but with purpose.

ONE LAST THING

This morning, which began like any morning,
My wife went running with the dog.
She tied her sneakers, secured the collar around his neck.

After they'd disappeared into the woods, the dog,
As was his habit, stopped to pee.
My wife looked off into the branches, which were laced with
   snow.
And though the leash was tight in her hand,
The collar fastened to the leash,
When she looked back the dog was gone.

How could she come home without the dog?
How could she explain not simply that he'd run away,
But that he'd vanished,
No shadow, no narrative,
A smudge of white against white snow?

Truthfully, I witnessed none of this.
But I can attest to the fact that when she returned,
The dog was trotting beside her.

No conclusions; observations.

I brewed the coffee, retrieved the paper from the stoop.

Without dislodging a single flake,

A cardinal settled on a branch.

THE HARBOR

1.

Slowly the harbor fills with fishing boats; the protagonist
Watches girls on the beach.
Every morning the same four girls, one with a bicycle.

The narrator explains that when you love one thing deeply, a
    person, a place,
Ultimately you love them all.
You know you're going to die, of course you do,
But you imagine a future, one that is a version of the past.
    What else could it be?

Your body, which since birth has served you well,
Continues to hold out its promise of both pleasure and pain.

Whom to prefer? The protagonist
Who understands nothing,
Or the narrator for whom everything is understood?

The slips stand empty, waiting for their boats.
The water follows the irregularities of the shoreline so a boat
at sea,
Half hidden by the fishing shacks,
May seem to be sailing through the middle of town.

2.

How could it be possible? How could earth last longer than
    ourselves,
Who, feeling there was room
To store so many treasures,
Had thrown sea and sky repeatedly away?

Never did it occur to us that death, its first assault,
Might occur this very afternoon,
This afternoon whose schedule, hour by hour,
Has been settled in advance.

We have hesitated over which car to take, which service to call,
We are in the car, the whole day lies before us—

And we have no suspicion that death,
Which all along has been growing inside us,
Has chosen precisely this day to make its appearance,
Just as we're crossing Edgemere Drive.

3.

The protagonist prepares for bed, and having slept,
Awakens the following morning.
A force that once looked after him
Abandons him, a force of which he'd never been aware.

He tries to speak to that force.
He bargains, tries to give it a name.
He imagines what he'd say if, being dead, he heard his
    daughters' voices.

If you are speaking to me, he'd assure them,
I am listening to you speak. Who's listening now?

Which is more mysterious, more inexplicable, dying or
    staying alive?
Which makes more sense, each cell in your body
Servile, following orders,
Or a few now liberated not to care?

The protagonist prepares for bed;
He closes his book, then closes his eyes.

Boats in the harbor. A little boy
For whom he buys a dish of ice cream.

4.

It is in sickness that we recognize, no matter the
circumstance, we're never alone.
That we are shackled to a body different from ourselves.

*Before your mind existed, before it needed to exist, you were
your body.*
By taking care of it, your mother took care of you.
*When by necessity your body was neglected, you learned to
take care of yourself.*

A body whom we have always known
But from whom we are worlds apart.

You wanted to be neglected;
You needed to invent your mind.

A body who has no knowledge of us,
Though he causes us pain.
A body to whom it is impossible to make ourselves understood.

In the mind, you're capable of soothing yourself
Not only when you're neglected, but when you're loved.

5.

Evenings, whenever I watched my daughters sleep, I felt like
    an angel.
I'd never seen an angel, but that's how I felt.

Immediately they smiled in the morning, but sometimes
    they cried;
I'd hold their tiny bodies against me.
Why are you crying? They couldn't say.

When I woke up from surgery,
I could open only one eye.
I could hear voices, but I couldn't see.
Come over here, I asked, so I can see you. Then I saw.

The Temple of Baal is gone forever,
Likewise the great stone Buddhas of Bamiyan.
Titian's *Battle of Spoleto*, Caravaggio's *Saint John*—all of
    them gone.

Often I'm asked if I'd return to where I came from,
Resume the life of the person I once was,
But the answer, any answer,
Implies a narrative
About the purpose of suffering.

6.

In the back of the closet is a suitcase filled with clothes.
Look how carefully the shirts have been folded,
How lovingly the handkerchiefs have been pressed,
Handkerchiefs that never dried an eye.

He might have wished for another season, longer or later,
    winter or summer,
It wouldn't matter which.
Hasn't he worked hard, harder than anyone?

The boats come in, the boats go out.
The docks are paved with starfish, which the fishermen discard.

Can there be any day but this?
Look, there is the sea, and there is the sky.

PASTORAL

Every morning people do exactly what I do.
They make their beds, they practice their lutes.
Then why am I so afraid?

Girls are stringing daisies,
Rearranging peaches in a china bowl.
Boys are sulking in the forest, thinking about death.

But after they've swept the cave,
Tidied up the pallet of rumpled ferns,
Out come the lutes, they play.
The birds begin to sing.

The girls are waiting
In the gallery, braiding ribbons
In each other's hair. Where are the boys?

I know it's been the longest year on record.
Our crutches are worn out.
For everyone, it's been the same.

But you know how this ends as well as I do.
The lutes come out,
The birds begin to sing,
The boys and girls are lying in the grass. If anything

Earth looks a little younger now.
I love you, earth.
What space I inhabit
You'll fill with water or sky.

Acknowledgments

My thanks to the editors of the following magazines, in which these poems originally appeared:

Birmingham Poetry Review: "Earthling"
Colorado Review: "The Hummingbird"
Little Star: "Pastoral"
The Nation: "Complaint"
The New Republic: "Huntington Meadow"
The New Yorker: "The Crocodile," "Suitcase"
Plume: "The Dishwasher"
Poetry: "Allegory," "Arcadia," "By the Same Author"
Raritan: "The Academy," "One Last Thing"
Salmagundi: "Lyric Knowledge," "Petite Maison"
The Threepenny Review: "Book Three," "Climate of Reason,"
   "The Harbor"

"Climate of Reason" is indebted to Flaubert's *Temptation of Saint Anthony*, Marion Milner's *On Not Being Able to Paint*, and Helen Waddell's *Desert Fathers*.

James Longenbach is the author of four previous collections of poems, including *The Iron Key* and *Draft of a Letter*, and of six books of literary criticism, including *The Virtues of Poetry* and *The Art of the Poetic Line*. His poems and his reviews of contemporary American poets have appeared in many magazines, including *The Nation, The New Yorker*, and the *New York Times Book Review*. The recipient of an Award in Literature from the American Academy of Arts and Letters, Longenbach teaches at the University of Rochester, where he is the Joseph H. Gilmore Professor of English.